D0275636

Plum

Plum

Tony Mitton

Illustrated by
Peter Bailey

SCHOLASTIC
PRESS

Scholastic Children's Books,
Commonwealth House, 1–19 New Oxford Street
London WC1A 1NU, UK
a division of Scholastic Ltd
London ~ New York ~ Toronto ~ Sydney ~ Auckland

First published by Scholastic Ltd, 1998

ISBN (hb) 0 590 54291 5
ISBN (pb) 0 590 54456 x

Typeset by Rowland Phototypesetting Ltd, Bury St Edmunds, Suffolk
Printed by Clays Ltd, St Ives plc

10 9 8 7 6 5 4 3 2 1

For Elizabeth, Doris, Guthrie and Dad
with love
T. M.

Contents

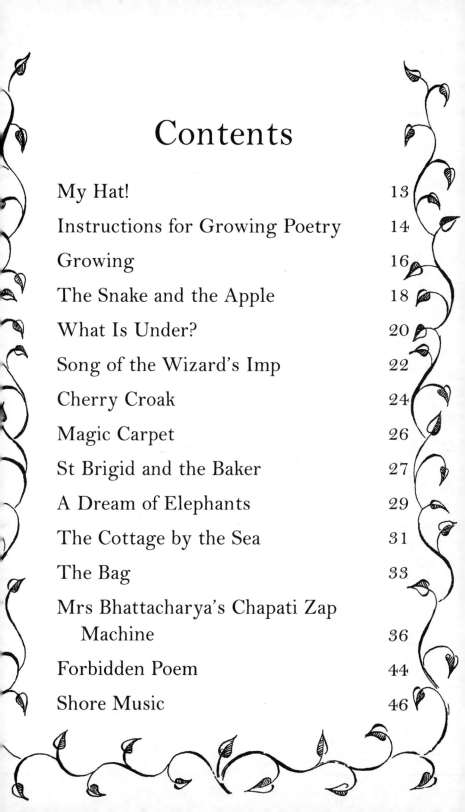

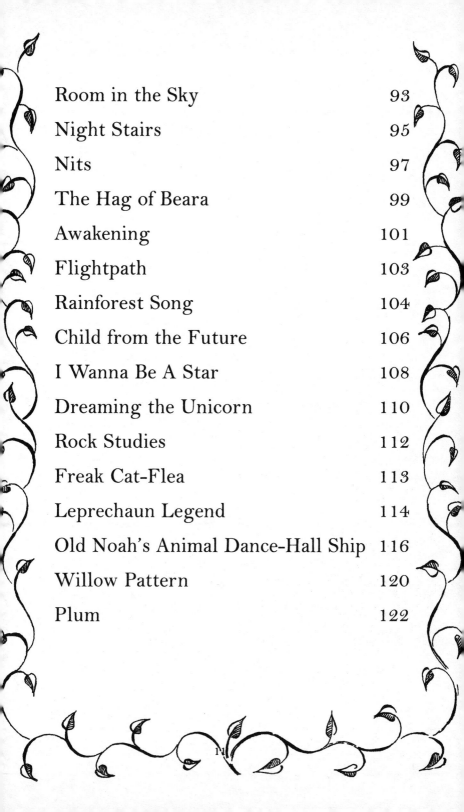

My Hat!

Here's my hat.
It holds my head,
the thoughts I've had
and the things I've read.

It keeps out the wind.
It keeps off the rain.
It hugs my hair
and warms my brain.

There's me below it,
the sky above it.
It's my lid.
And I love it.

Instructions for Growing Poetry

(found on the back of the packet)

Shut your eyes.
Open your mind.
Look inside.
What do you find?
Something funny?
Something sad?
Something beautiful,
mysterious, mad?
Open your ears.
Listen well.
A word or phrase
begins to swell?
Catch its rhythm.
Hold its sound.
Gently, slowly
roll it round.
Does it please you?
Does it tease you?

Does it ask
to grow and spread?
Now those little
words are sprouting
poetry
inside your head.

Growing

Today
you may be small.
But one day
you'll be tall,
like me,
maybe taller.
You won't
fit into your bed.
Your hat
won't fit on your head.
Your feet
will fill up the floor.
You'll have to bend down
to come through the door.
You'll be able to reach
to the highest shelf,
(and I can't do that now,
myself).
Out in the country
the tallest trees
will scratch your ankles

and tickle your knees.
Up in the clouds,
yes, way up there,
the eagles will nest
in your craggy hair.
But they'd better soon find
a safer place
because soon your head
will be up in space.

So I hope you won't be too proud
to bend down
and say hello
to your old home-town.
And I hope it won't drive you
utterly mad
to visit your tiny
Mum and Dad.

The Snake and the Apple

The snake lay up in the apple tree
out of the heat of the day.
"There's nothing to fear from an apple,
 my dear,"
I heard him slyly say.

He curled his coils around the branch
and looked with a lidless eye.
"It's sweet, for sure, whether eaten raw
or baked in a nice hot pie."

The snake lay up in the apple tree
out of the light of the sun.
"There's enough in the tree for you and
 me,
and enough for everyone."

He licked at a rosy apple
with a smile and a slippery hiss.
"You've nothing to fear from an apple,
    my dear.
Just take a bite. It's bliss."

This poem is based on the Bible story where the serpent
tempts Eve with the forbidden fruit. (Genesis, Chapter 3,
Old Testament.)

What Is Under?

What is under the grass, Mummy,
what is under the grass?
Roots and stones and rich soil
where the loamy worms pass.

What is over the sky, Mummy,
what is over the sky?
Stars and planets and boundless space,
but never a reason why.

What is under the sea, Mummy,
what is under the sea?
Weird and wet and wondrous things,
too deep for you and me.

What is under my skin, Mummy,
what is under my skin?
Flesh and blood and a frame of bones
and your own dear self within.

Once, when my daughter was about four and her
mother was gardening, she suddenly asked with great
seriousness, "What is under the grass, Mummy?" This
question kept coming back to me and gradually grew
into a poem.

Song of the Wizard's Imp

Catch me if you can,
I'm a whisper of air,
a splinter of sunlight
that's gone if you stare.

Catch me if you can,
I'm a shadowy patch,
a rustle of cobweb
that's gone if you snatch.

Catch me if you can,
but be sure that you dare,
for I nestle to rest
in a wizard's warm hair.

Yes, catch me if you can,
but be warned I am weird,
for I settle to sleep
in the wizard's white beard.

Oh, catch me if you can,
but don't wake the wizard.
He'll glare and he'll growl
and you'll end up a lizard.

It was often thought that witches and wizards
had "familiars", strange little animals or
creatures who kept them company and
helped them with their magic.

Cherry Croak

(*or* Raiding the Wizard's Kitchen)

Cor!
I wonder what this is for?
It's all red and fizzy,
just like cherry coke
(except for the smoke. . .)

Hmmmm. . .
cool as ice.
Mmmmm. . .
smells nice.
Think, maybe
I'll try a sip.
Oooh! Bubbles bursting
on my lip –
Pop! Pop! Pop!

Heeeeey! Everything's taller.

Oh, no. It's me that's getting smaller.

Oooh! *Hop! Hop! Hop!*

Well, I'm blowed!

I've turned into a toad.

That was no coke.

And this is no joke.

Croak, croak, croak...

Magic Carpet

Magic carpet,
your bright colours
delight the eye.

Your moons and stars
and midnight blues
sing of the sky.

Magic carpet,
kept in the cupboard,
I hear you sigh.

Let me unroll
your magic pattern
and help you fly.

St Brigid and the Baker

As Brigid was walking
the old narrow track
she passed by a baker
with bread in his sack.

She put out a hand
from the fold of her cloak,
and these are the words
she softly spoke:

*"Please give me a loaf
for my sisters and me,
and we'll share it tonight
as we sit to our tea."*

But the baker, he muttered
and shook a mean head.
*"If you want to eat, sister,
then bake your own bread."*

She looked in his eyes then,
but all that she found
was a stare that was hard
as the stones on the ground.

So Brigid passed quietly
along the hard track
as the bread turned to stone
on the baker's back.

St Brigid of Ireland has many miracle stories
told about her. Often these show her to be
kind and generous. Sometimes she manages
to increase food and drink to feed
unexpected guests. For it was said that, as a
young cow-girl, Brigid could draw more milk
from a cow than anyone else. She had a
special way with the animals.

A Dream of Elephants

I dreamed a dream of elephants.
I cannot tell you why.
But in my dream I saw the herd
go slowly walking by.

They moved beneath a blazing sun,
through rising dust and heat.
They made their solemn journey
on strong and silent feet.

And as I watched, the steady herd
walked slowly, sadly by,
until I stood, amazed, alone,
beneath a silent sky.

I watched them as they moved away.
I watched as they walked on.
They merged into the heat and dust
till all of them were gone.

I dreamed a dream of elephants.
I cannot tell you why.
But in my dream I saw the herd
go slowly walking by.

I read somewhere that the African elephants have
less and less room to live in their natural state. Even
in that huge continent it seems that they are running
out of space.

The Cottage by the Sea

If you go there by day,
out to the ruined cottage
that sits on the cliff,
all you will find is silence.

Perhaps the wind
will pick at a broken shutter,
or maybe a gull
will cry as it flies overhead.

But if you go there by day,
all you will find is stillness
except for a scurry of ants
or maybe a thrush
cracking a snail on a rock.

But if you go there by night
when the moon is low
and the mist drifts in from the sea,
you may find lights and music,
noises of joy and laughter
left over from lives gone by.

But then if you step through the door
to join with the fun,
everything vanishes, everything closes.
You'll find yourself standing alone,
amazed in the darkness,
with everything silent
and only the wind at your ear.

The Bag

(for Catherine Byron)

Nobody comes to the gate.
Because of the bag.

Nobody knocks at the door.
Because of the bag.

Nobody enters the house.
Because of the bag.

Nobody sits in the room.
Because of the bag.

Nobody kindles the fire.
Because of the bag.

Because of the bag.

The bag in the hearth.

The bag in the hearth
with horns and bones.

The bag with beads
and burrs and stones.

The bag with rue
and a sprig of thyme:

a strange collection
of things to rhyme,

of things to finger
and things to tell,

and things to cast
their silent spell.

And nobody comes to the house.
Because of the bag.

This poem came out of a writing class held by the poet Catherine Byron. To get us writing, she produced a bag with a mixture of things in it. I noticed that the names of many of the things rhymed with each other. This gave me the idea of a kind of spell-bag that a country wise-woman might have made.

Mrs Bhattacharya's Chapati Zap Machine

You've heard of slapstick? Well, this poem is chapatstick!

Mrs Bhattacharya's Chapati Zap Machine
is marvellous, amazing. It's the best there's
  ever been.
It sizzles hot chapatis at a most amazing rate,
then flicks them spinning through the air to
  land upon your plate.

Mrs Bhattacharya's Chapati Zap Machine
has buttons, knobs and levers in blue and red
  and green.
It mixes fine chapati flavours: peppered,
  spiced or plain,
then shoots them out in showers like a hot
  chapati rain.

Now Mrs Bhattacharya's machine is very new,
so even Mrs B can't say for sure what it will do.
And yes, it rather looks as if she's getting in a
    flurry
as 20 hot chapatis make a landing in the curry.

But Mrs Bhattacharya's a brilliant
    engineer.
She tinkers with a spanner and she listens
    with an ear.
She twiddles with a lever and she fiddles with
    a dial.
"I think that puts the trouble right,"she
    whispers with a smile.

Mrs Bhattacharya's Chapati Zap Machine
is going to the Palace by Appointment to the
    Queen.
The Queen wants hot chapatis for a royal
    dinner guest,
and someone's told her Mrs B's chapatis are
    the best.

Mrs Queen and all her guests are sitting
  down to dine.
The President of Zarnia has come, and all
  looks fine.
A bell is rung, the doors swing wide, and
  suddenly is seen. . .
Yes! Mrs Bhattacharya's Chapati Zap
  Machine!

Mrs Bhattacharya is pressing Button Blue.
The ground begins to tremble. . . The Zap
  Machine goes Phooooo!
Now Mrs Bhattacharya is pressing Button
  Red
as 6 big hot chapatis flip out swiftly past her
  head.

One flies up and perches on the crystal
  chandelier.
Another settles neatly on an Admiral's left
ear.
And one with lots of butter, a lovely golden
  brown,
flies straight toward the Queen and
  punctures, PLOP! upon her crown.

One attacks a General and slaps him on the
  head –
he snorts into his sherry and his face goes
  very red.
Another meets a Duchess and causes her
  distress
by landing on her shoulder and sliding down
  her dress.

But one especial big one, the largest of the lot,
all seasoned, spiced and buttered, all round
  and steaming hot,
performs the worst thing possible, a terrible
  disgrace:
It squelches on the President of Zarnia's
  solemn face!

Mrs Bhattacharya shuts down her Zap
  Machine.
Disaster such as this the royal guests have
  never seen.
They wait to hear the anger of the Queen,
  who shakes her head.
But then, to their surprise, the words they
  hear are these instead:

"Hurrah!", shouts Zarnia's president, "And
   double hip hooray
for Mrs Bhattacharya's Chapati Cabaret!
Is this a British Bunfight? I've heard of
   these before.
Keep going, Bhattacharya. I'd love to play
   some more!"

Mrs Bhattacharya looks straight toward
   the Queen,
who nods, "Yes . . . start it up again, your
   . . . 'cabaret' machine."
Next moment Zarnia leaps up high to catch
   a fast chapat,
then throws it in the air and shrieks,
   "A splendid catch – HOWZAT!"

Then bit by bit the guests forget they're
   grown-up and polite.
They start to dodge and duck and catch,
   like children, with delight.
And bishops, bigwigs, baronets and butlers
   … everyone
begin to feel, since they were small, they
   haven't had such fun.

And now, to cut a story short, a party with
   the Queen
is really quite a different thing from what it
   used to mean.
The guests all turn up gleefully with faces
   bright and keen …
for Mrs Bhattacharya's Chapati Zap
   Machine.

So Mrs Bhattacharya is famous in the end,
and if you plan a party soon please don't
   forget to send
for Mrs Bhattacharya who, as I've just
   heard tell,
is setting her machine to pump out
   poppadoms as well.

It's fabulous, it's marvellous, it's big and
   bright and clean.
Its buttons, knobs and levers are blue and
   red and green.
It's chosen by Appointment to Her Majesty
   the Queen.
It's Mrs Bhattacharya's Chapati Zap Machine.

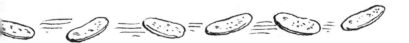

Forbidden Poem

This poem is not for children.
Keep out!
There is a big oak door
in front of this poem.
It's locked.
And on the door is a notice
in big red letters.
It says: Any child who enters here
will never be the same again.
WARNING. KEEP OUT.

But what's this?
A key in the keyhole.
And what's more,
nobody's about.

"Go on. Look,"
says a little voice
inside your head.
"Surely a poem
cannot strike you dead?"

You turn the key.
The door swings wide.
And then you witness
what's inside.

And from that day
you'll try in vain.
You'll never be the same again.

Shore Music

When the wind is calm
and the moon is full
and the waters softly swing,

you may see the mermaids
sit by the shore
as they comb their hair and sing.

Your ears may long
for their strange sea-song,
but do not tread too near.

At the slightest sound
of a foot on the ground
they will dip . . . dip . . . disappear.

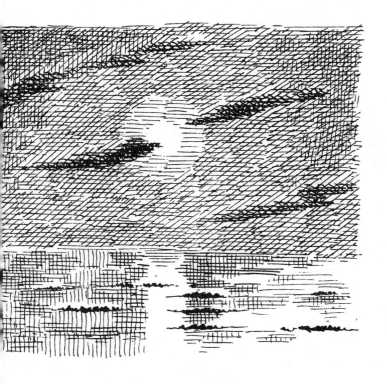

Early
Walkman

(5 million years ago)

Some people say that human-like creatures
began walking upright on two legs about
5 million years ago. Perhaps even then they
began to feel the need for a personal
sound system? This poem, streetwise
before streets were invented, is intended
to be spoken in a deep, slow growl.

Fasten sea-shell
on to each ear.

Listen. Amazing!
What me hear?

Sound of water,
wind and rain
washing about
inside my brain.

Stand on two legs.
Walk along.
Listening to
that sea-shell song.

Ballad of the Little Boat

– a landsman sings to a nymph of the sea

If love were but a little boat
we'd launch it with the tide.
We'd sit beneath the swelling sail
and cross the ocean wide.

We'd travel to the distant west,
our hearts a-brim and bold.
We'd leave behind the chilly lands
and find the Isles of Gold.

And when we once arrived there
we'd step upon the shore
to pluck the pleasures of the place
and more and more and more.

And once we both were sated
we'd stretch upon the strand
to marvel at the jewelled stars
that spill like silver sand,

and listen to the mermaids
whose songs are strange and swell,
and thrill to all the stories
the whispering waves would tell.

But, oh, I am a landsman,
the sea is vast and deep.
Its squalls and storms are terrible.
Its waves are stern and steep.

Indeed, I am a landsman,
with house and family.
My life is firmly locked on land,
I cannot sail the sea.

So love must be a little boat
that sleeps upon the beach.
And, oh, those distant Golden Isles
are dreams, and out of reach.

The Selkie Bride

From around the coasts of Scotland and Ireland come many old tales about the selkie-folk or seal-people. In some of these stories the selkies have the power to shed their skins and come on land to be amongst human beings. To return to the water as seals they have to put their skins back on. The ballad that follows is a version of one of the better-known selkie stories.

Young Donallan lived alone
with the sound of the sea and the wind's wild
  moan,
and the hiss of the kettle, the sigh of the peat,
with a cat in his lap and a dog at his feet.

Young Donallan spread his net.
He landed the fish that he could get.
He grew his cabbage in a scant croft patch,
and he caulked his boat and he roped his
  thatch.

On the seventh day of the high Spring tide
his heart grew full and he stretched and
    sighed.
So he walked the length of the lonely strand
to the chafe of the surf on the soft sea sand.

Young Donallan tuned his ear
to the cry of the gulls on the salt sea air.
But above the birds and the fall of the flood
there rose a sound that swelled his blood.

Down on the rocks a selkie sang,
and he drank the song till his senses rang.
He gazed at the sight of her glimmering
    there
with her graceful form and her winnowing
    hair.

He knew the lore and the ways of old
from the talk, and the tales his father told.
So he seized the skin that lay by her side,
crying, "Selkie, I take you to be my bride."

She begged for the skin, on her bended knee,
for without it she could not return to the sea.
But her eyes were dark and her skin was soft,
and Donallan led her back to his croft.

Young Donallan and his selkie bride
lived in the croft to the tune of the tide.
She stitched his shirt and she baked his bread
and she lay by his side in the old box bed.

She bore him children, one, two, three.
Their eyes were as soft as the seals' of the sea.
They loved their mother with her gentle ways
but they knew her sigh and her sad sea gaze.

And they felt in their hearts there was
    something wrong
for her voice was sweet but she sang no song.
Whenever she soothed them to sleep at night
her eyes were kind but her lips pressed tight.

* * *

It was on a day when the wind was wild
and Donallan was out with the eldest child,
that the Selkie Bride was baking bread
when all of a sudden the youngest said,

"Early this morning while the family slept
I followed our father out where he crept.
He loosened a stone in the old croft wall
and he took from the hollow a sleek grey
    caul.

"He oiled and smoothed that supple skin,
then he folded it tight and put it back in.
Now tell me, Mother, oh spell to me
the meaning of this mystery."

But his mother, never a word she said.
She found the skin and she left her bread.
Then she led the children to the edge of the
    land
where the waters lap at the silver sand.

"Now, listen, my dears, oh listen to me.
Your mother's home is here in the sea.
It was here in Spring, at the height of the
    tide,
your father took me to be his bride.

"And though it tear at your mother's heart,
it's here on the shore that we must part."
She shook her skin and she put it on.
Then she fell to the waves and she was
    gone.

When they told their father, he scarcely
    stirred.
He gave a sigh, but he spoke no word.
For he knew that a selkie, such as she,
must come at last to her home in the sea.

So Donallan lived in the small thatched croft,
with his children three and their eyes so soft.
But whenever in Spring the tides rose high
and a round moon rode in the cool night sky,

they would hear the music, clear and strong,
the sound of their mother's selkie song,
and they knew she was near, in the swing of
   the sea,
where the waters roll and the seal swim free.

And from that time, in the midst of the storm,
they were safe from the waves that spoil and
   harm.
And whoever was of their selkie brood,
their boats stayed sound and their catch
   was good.

Bubble Songs

1
If you blow
I will grow
to a trembling ball.

I'm a bubble of breath
in a shimmering shawl.

If you lift
I will drift
like a wisp of the air.

Then I'll burst with a gasp
and I'm simply not there.

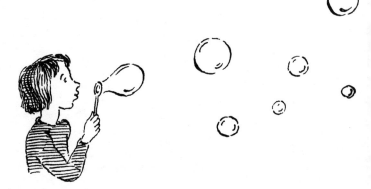

2

I am only
a bubble,
the ghost of a ball.
If I'm caught then I'm nought,
I am nothing at all.

I am only
a bubble,
a shimmering sphere.

If I land on your hand
I shall soon disappear.

Secret Passage

Inside this poem
is a secret door.
You cannot see it
but it's there for sure.

Behind this word
is a little lever.
Take firm hold
and give a little heave, a

panel will open
to reveal a stair
leading down to . . .
I wonder where?

Down these steps
it's dark as night,
so take this torch
'cause we'll need some light.

Here at the bottom
is a dusty door.
This is getting interesting,
more and more. . .

Fumble at the wall,
find a small catch,
give a little tug,
release the latch,

give it a push,
the door creaks wide,
tread in carefully
and you're inside.

Inside what?
Well, it's a sort of
vault full of all the things
you've ever thought of.

Now this is the kind
of adventure I love –
but what's that noise
on the page above?

Ulp, oh no …
come and have a look.
We've gone and got trapped here.
Someone's shut the book!

The Alphabattle

The poet sat with writer's rage
and spilled his thoughts upon the page,
but as his pen flew swiftly writing
the wriggling letters fell to fighting:

A got axed and B got bent.
C got coshed. D took a dent.
E was erased while F took flight.
G got gored and H lost height.
I got ink-stained. J was jerked.
K was kicked and L just lurked.
M got mangled. N got nailed.
O turned over. P just paled.
Q went queasy. R got rapped.
S got straightened. T got tapped.
U went under. V went vapid.
W wailed,
and X made an exit (rapid!)
Y just yelped and left the fray.
Z zipped off to run away.

No more letters. No more text.
The poet cried, "Whatever next . . .?"
He shook his head and looked aghast,
but his readers murmured, "Peace at last!"

The Minstrel and the Maid

(overheard on a cottage door-step)

This is a courtship lyric. The plain print shows the
minstrel's voice and the italics show the clever
maid's replies.

I'll strike you a strain
from a silver string.

*I'll do you a dance
that's fit for a king.*

I'll breathe you an air
on a flute of gold.

*I'll tell you a tale
that's wise and old.*

I'll fiddle you a jig
that's wild and funny.

I'll find you an almond
dipped in honey.

I'll tickle you a rhythm
on a magic drum.

I'll show you a taste
of a sugarplum.

I'll pipe you a tune
on a whistle of wood.

I'll bake you a cake
that's warm and good.

I'll sing my song
in a strong, clear voice.

I'll give you anything.
Take your choice.

little red
typewriter ditty

little red typewriter
sitting so neat
let me please

tap out a lyric
upon your fleet
black and white keys

tick with your typeface
and ding your sweet
end-of-line bell

think of the poems
each time that we meet
we shall tell

reel out your ribbon
and roll a clean sheet
on your drum

print out the words
with your delicate beat
as they come

When she was having a junk clearance,
one of my friends gave my children an old,
red Olivetti Valentine typewriter. I was so
delighted by this little, old-fashioned
writing machine that I sat down to write a
poem for it. As the model was called
"Valentine" and it was bright red, it had
to be a valentine poem. The rhythm tries
to echo the staccato beat of a manual
typewriter, which may now very soon
be forgotten.

Nightwriter

(for the snail)

Slow secretary of darkness writing in
  rambling, leisurely line,
moonlight illuminator, scribe of the silver
  shine,
picaresque calligrapher, tracing the tracts
  of the night,
poet of ponderous silence, what did you
  write?

Curious patterning, casual and cursive
  trail,
text of intuitive, sensitive, intricate snail,
subtle and secretly hatched from the skull of
  the shell,
what is your glistening message? What does
  it tell?

Asking Anansi

Sometimes spider, sometimes man, Anansi is a
popular trickster character in Caribbean
stories. He has a whole group of stories
named after him. To me, making stories,
spinning yarns and weaving webs all have things
in common. This poem is meant to be spoken
in a slow, relaxed Caribbean drawl.

"Anansi,
tell me. . .
what you
gonna do
with so much thread?
Don't it tangle up
yo' head?"

Anansi smiled,
and this is what
he said:

"Gonna take it. . .
easy. . .
No tangle.

Just dangle.

Go knit meself
a hammock-bed.
Hang it high
and rest me head.
Catch a fly
and get me fed.

"Then maybe,
when things
are hunky-dory,
lie back,
dream a bit,
and knit
meself a story."

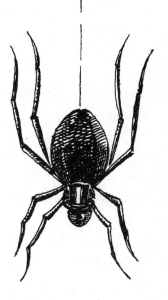

Mrs Rummage's Muddle-Up Shop

When I tried to ask for a lollipop
in Mrs Rummage's Muddle-Up Shop,
she stopped and said, "I think I might. . .
"Let's see. . . I saw one here last night.

"Now, just where did that lollipop go. . .?
Where exactly. . .? I don't know.

"Oh, dear. This really just won't do. . .
Is there something else I can get for you?"

And when I said, "I think it's there. . ."
she just looked blank and scratched her hair.

"Now where," she said, "in a Muddle-Up
  Shop,
would you go looking for a lollipop?"
And she pulled things out and let them go
as she started to rummage high and low:

"Over here with the diving gear?

"Under there with the underwear?

"Up on top with the soda pop?

"Down below where the loo-rolls go?

"In that box with the fancy socks?

"In this tin with the buttons in?

"Way up high with the rhubarb pie?

"On those racks with the plastic macs?

"By the telly with the raspberry jelly?

"Near the jar where the pickles are?

"Under the stairs with the folding chairs?

"In the bin with the brollies in?"

And she reached up high and she
    rummaged low
but she wouldn't hear when I tried to
    show.

"Oh, dear," she'd say, "I'm sure it's here.
How *can* a lollipop disappear?

"Let's have a *really* good look round.
That's the way that a lollipop's found…"

It's then I had to shout, "PLEASE STOP!
I JUST WANT TO BUY *THAT*
  LOLLIPOP!"

"Oh, that!" she said, "Why, goodness me!
You can have *that* lollipop just for free...

"That is..." she said, with slight distress,
"if you'll help me clear up all this mess...!"

The Histon Boulder

(Moses Carter's Stone)

Moses Carter, late of Histon,
seven foot plus and strong as a piston,
mustered strength of arm and shoulder,
hoisted up the Histon Boulder,
covered the distance (bless my soul!)
down to The Boot from The Ballast Hole.

Moses moved that massive stone
unassisted, quite alone,
just for a wager, just for a bet.
No one else has moved it yet.
There by The Boot it's still to be seen,
a step or so from the village green.

Moses Carter, great of height,
fond of children, kind, polite,
munched his dumplings, chewed his beef,
passed away to general grief.
If giants were all so calm, so tame,
they wouldn't earn so bad a name.

Moses Carter, dead and gone,
has left behind his heavy stone.
Nothing else, apart from that,
but a single boot and a stovepipe hat.
In Histon Churchyard now he lies
in a grave they dug him, giant size.

Moses Carter's stone can still be seen in the garden of The
Boot public house, Histon, Cambridgeshire. The distance
from The Ballast Hole to The Boot is by my reckoning a
good half-mile by way of the road. Moses died in the 1860s
and, according to local history, is buried in Histon churchyard.
On my visit there I couldn't find a headstone for him. Perhaps
he could not afford one, so he may be glad for this poem to
serve instead.

These Old Shoes

These old shoes
have scuffs and stains.
They've trudged through snow
and pelting rains.

They've tramped their way
to school each dawn.
And now they're wrinkled,
lined and worn.

But these old shoes
have danced with glee.
They've clambered up
our Climbing Tree.

They may have cracks
and fraying laces.
But these old shoes
have won at races.

They're down at heel
with thinning soles.
But once these shoes
were scoring goals.

They've pushed at pedals,
trod the street.
They've tapped in time
to music's beat.

They've stood at bus-stops
for an age.
They've stamped in puddles
(and with rage).

And if I listed
all they'd done,
this poem would simply
run and run.

But though they once
were bright and neat,
and though they've stoutly
served my feet,

they're battered now
and much too tight,
and so it's time
to say goodnight.

Let's lift the lid
from off the bin
and gently, softly
drop them in.

Puzzled Pea

I'm just a pea
in a plain pea pod.
But there's something about me
that's odd.

For, although like the others,
I'm a plain, green pea,
they are all *them*. . .
while I'm *me*.

Stone Circles

The ones
who set these stones
were shrewd, star-wise.

They knew the skies.

And plotted points
where sun and moon
would sink and rise.

They knew to measure,
calculate and place.

Transported massive weight
through tracts of space.

But why they hauled these stones
and set them so,
we only guess,
we cannot surely know.

Their thoughts, their reasons,
their intense belief
have blown away
on vanished winds,
light as a leaf.

The meaning's lost.
The flesh is gone.
All we have now are stones,
standing abandoned here
like remnant bones.

This poem is especially about Stonehenge, but
refers also to the many other stone circles to be
found in Britain and Western Europe.

Green Man Lane

As I went walking down Green Man Lane
I met a stranger there.
His clothes were all of foliage
and tangled was his hair.

He did not pause for pleasantry
nor bid me how-d'ye-do.
He only stood with eyes of wood
that pierced me sharply through.

The leaves crept close around me.
The earth pressed at my feet.
I felt the breeze upon my skin,
my heart's insistent beat.

Never a word the stranger spoke,
though his stare was keen and clear.
But the leaves around us rustled,
and my blood ran thick with fear.

And the leaves around us shivered
as a sudden silence fell.
And I felt the life of the ragged wood
in that dark and greeny cell.

I felt the thirst of each living leaf
as it lapped at the air for breath.
And I felt the search of each striving root
as it sifted life from death.

A scent of blood and fear sprang up,
a grip of beak and jaw.
And slow things moved in rich decay
beneath the forest floor.

Then a small bird sang out sharply
as the sunlight filtered through.
So I stepped out into the meadow
beneath a sky of blue.

And I saw how the field of bearded wheat
had grown from green to gold.
Then I thought of the man in the leafy coat,
with his look so keen and bold.

But whether the sun be shining bright
or the hedge be wet with rain,
I'll hesitate before I pass
along that lane again.

For those readers who have not yet met the Green Man, he is a well-known figure in British folklore. He is often thought to stand for the power of growth in nature. The Green Man's name is preserved on many pub and street signs. His image can be seen in churches all over Europe, carved in wood or stone.

Elegant Elephant Delicatessen

(once visited, never forgotten)

Come to the Elephant Delicatessen.
Sample the delicate elephant treats.
Savour the flavour of elephant edibles.
Taste what the elegant elephant eats.

Come to the Elephant Delicatessen.
Tickle your trunk with a truffle or two.
Toy with a tit-bit of tree-leaf in aspic,
Oh, Epicurean Elephant, you!

Come to the Elephant Delicatessen.
Elephant aliments spill from our shop.
Pick up a packet of Pachyderm Poppadoms.
Sip at a schooner of Elephant Pop.

Here in the Elephant Delicatessen
Are exquisite rarities gathered from far.
So come for a great gastronomical lesson.
We're just by the Elephant Superbazaar.

(PS We are serving free Eleffervessence
delivered today from our Elephant Spa.)

Tree Song

City of whispers,
symphony of sighs,
intricate embroidery
sampling the skies.

Machinery of nature,
factory of air,
delirious dancer
dishevelling her hair.

Room in the Sky

Way up high
is my room in the sky.
If you want to visit
you'll have to fly.

Floating in air
is my favourite lair.
Another way up's
by invisible stair.

If you manage to knock
you're in for a shock.
There's neither a handle,
a hinge nor a lock.

And furthermore
there isn't a door.
There aren't any windows,
there isn't a floor.

And what sends you reeling:
there isn't a ceiling!
It gives you a very
peculiar feeling.

So can you say where
is my room in the air?
Perhaps it's a fiction
which just isn't there?

There isn't a trace?
It's just empty space?
For a room it's a very
mysterious place.

However, to me
it's a fine place to be.
So come up and visit,
I'm making some tea.

Night Stairs

In medieval cathedrals, such as Wells in
Somerset, there are old stone staircases
worn to a curve on each tread by the
steady procession of feet down the
centuries.

The feet of the monk
will tread, will tread
on the midnight stair
by candle led
as he makes his way
from his austere bed
to the choir
where the holy words
are said
and the chants are chanted,
incense burned
till the office ends

and his steps are turned
back to the tread
of the midnight stair
where each step curves
with the steady wear
of the tread, the tread
of feet, of feet
through years of steady
slow repeat
as the steps of the monk
are neatly led
back to the sleep
of his austere bed.

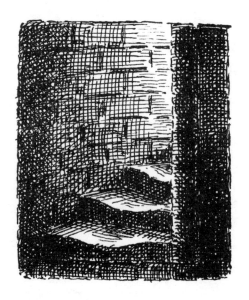

Nits

If you're scratching your head to bits
you could have nits.

And if you've got nits
you need to give your head a blitz.

You can get kits
to deal with nits.

But if it can help it,
a nit
      never quits.
It just sits
        tight
until night.
And then it might

    bite.

Yes, having nits
can drive you out of your wits.
They're the pits.
You're better off

with the squits!

I wrote this poem from scratch. You could try writing
one too, if you get the itch.

The Hag of Beara

Old hag walking
through weather and wind,
where are you headed
and what's in your mind?

I head for the sunset
across the sea
where the body is light
and the mind blows free.

Old hag hooded
and bent of back,
what do you bear
in your stony sack?

The woes of the world
on my back I bear.
When I reach my rest
they'll be light as air.

Old hag walking
the track alone,
what do you tell
with your song of stone?

The words on my lips
sing sure of the sun
which will warm my bones
when the journey's done.

Old hag walking
westward forever,
spelled in stone
and worn by weather.

If you travel down from Kilcatherine churchyard, just across the bay
from Eyeries on the Beara Peninsula in Southern Ireland, you can see
a strange stone that looks like an old woman with a sack on her back.
She appears to be walking out to sea, out to the west. It is said that
this is The Hag of Beara, the writer of one of the oldest poems in the
Irish Language. Some say she turned herself to stone, rather than take
on the new incoming religion brought by the Christian Fathers. I like
to think that she is heading steadily for the Isles of the Blest, that
golden place that Celtic legend says we go to when we die. These
isles are far out to the west, beyond the sunset.

Awakening

The Buddha sat silently
under a tree.
He sat and he waited
determinedly.

He sat like a statue
and scarcely stirred.
Out of his lips
came never a word.

He sat through the hours
of an Orient night,
and, just at the edges
of opening light,

up in the heaven,
so sharp and so far,
glimmered the spark
of a wakening star.

Sitting in stillness,
the sight that he saw
pierced him through
to the innermost core.

And all he could say
in his moment of bliss
was simply and purely,
"What is this?"

The story has been passed down that the Buddha
(Siddhartha Gautama) achieved a sudden and
powerful experience of understanding after many
years of study and practice. Exhausted by the
efforts he had made to get to grips with the
meaning of his life, he gave up and sat down in
meditation under the Bhodi tree, vowing not to
get up until some answer presented itself to him.
After sitting all night in meditation he caught sight
of the morning star rising. The clarity and power
of the moment that followed is sometimes called,
in English, his Enlightenment (or Awakening). In
spite of his already great learning and wisdom, all
he could say in response to the experience was,
"What is this?"

Flightpath

The reason why
the fly
annoys me,
as it does,
is that,
however hard I try,
I can't ignore its buzz.

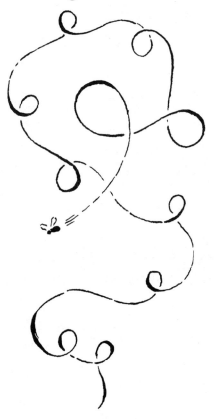

Rainforest Song

(for the people)

Forest, my mother,
feed me your fruit.
Forest, my father,
trace me my root.
Forest, my shelter,
spread me your shade,
as I walk in the glow
of your green forest glade.

Forest of whispers
and intricate ways,
Forest of spirits
that slip through your maze,
Forest of mystery,
subtle and deep,
you glide like a snake
through my waking and sleep.

Forest, the home
of my eye and my hand,
Forest, the meaning
I understand,
Forest, the ground
where I place my tread,
where I breathe my being
and pillow my head,

Forest, the world
I depend upon,
where will I walk
when my Forest has gone?

For many of the peoples of the rainforests, the
forest has been their entire world, providing them
with everything. It is giver & taker of life, material &
spiritual in its nature. As the forests are hacked back
by modern ways, so the ways of life of the rainforest
peoples are gradually destroyed.

Child from the Future

Child from the future, why do you stare at me
deep from your sorrowful eyes?
Why do you gaze with wonder
at the sight of our earth and skies?

Child from the future, why are you thin
and why do you seem so old?
Why do you walk so slowly,
and why do you shiver with cold?

Child from the future, why do you tremble
and why do you fill me with dread?
The child from the future sadly spoke
and these are the words she said:

"The air of your world is alive with birds
and your oceans are teeming with fish.
There is bread on your table and milk in
    your jug.
There are apples and nuts in your dish.

"If the world really was once like this
why did you throw it away?"
Then the child from the future melted
  slowly
back to her world of grey.

I Wanna Be A Star

I wanna be a star.
I wanna go far.
I wanna drive around
in a big red car.
I said yeah yeah yeah
I wanna be a star.

I wanna be a hit.
I wanna be it.
I wanna see my name
all brightly lit.
I said yeah yeah yeah
I wanna be a hit.

I wanna be the scene.
I wanna be on screen.
I wanna make the cover
of a magazine.
I said yeah yeah yeah
I wanna be the scene.

I wanna be a star.
I wanna be a star.
But I've only got a job
in a burger bar –
so far…

Dreaming the Unicorn

I dreamed I saw the Unicorn
last night.
It rippled through the forest,
pearly white,
breathing a moonlit silence.

Its single horn
stood shining like a lance.
I saw it toss its head
and snort and prance
and paw the midnight air.
Its mane was like a mass
of silver hair.

My mind was wild, unclear.
I could not think or speak.
Above my head, I heard the branches creak
and then, from where I stood,
I watched it flicker off into the wood,
into the velvet space between the trees.

A sudden rush of rapid midnight breeze,
that felt both chill and deep,
awoke me from my sleep,
and there upon the pillow by my head
I found a strand of shining silver thread.

I kept that strand of mane,
I keep it, still,
inside a box upon my window sill.
And when the world hangs heavy
on my brain,
it helps me dream the Unicorn again.

Rock Studies

(Eyeries Beach, West Cork, Ireland, 5th August
1994) 3 variations on a quatrain

a jagged rock
on a pebbled beach
that waits for lapping waves
to reach

a ragged rock
on a stony shore
that waits for the wear
of the soft sea claw

a haggard rock
on a hem of land
that waits for the fray
of the sea's slow hand

Freak Cat-Flea

Hullo, pussies,
come and see.
I'm the heftiest ever
feline flea.
I'm somewhat fat
and six foot three.
So I pity the cat
that catches me.

Our cat Tiggy sometimes picks up cat-fleas.
I'm glad she hasn't come across this one.

Leprechaun Legend

Leprechaun little
with cheek so ripe
sits by the hedgerow
smoking his pipe.
His tiny little hammer
goes *tap tap tap.*
Did you ever see
such a strange little chap?

Leprechaun little
sits mending a boot.
Leprechaun little
makes lots of loot.
Catch him by the collar,
hold him tight.
Hear him holler,
feel him fight.

Leprechaun little
has treasure, I'm told.
Deep in the earth
there's a crock of gold.
Squeeze him, tease him,
make him tell.
Feel him wriggle,
hear him yell.

Leprechaun little
is bright as pins.
He never loses,
always wins.
Leprechaun vanishes,
he's just not there.
Only his laughter
echoes in the air. . .

You can meet the Leprechaun in Irish folk
tales. No one ever gets to catch him, and if
they try he usually makes a fool of them.

Old Noah's Animal Dance-Hall Ship

Bang! Bang! Bang! Hey, what's that row?
Old Noah's building a dance-hall now!
It looks like a cabin on top of a boat
and we can't help wondering, Will it float?

Well, the rain came down on the dance-hall
  ship
while the animals learned to hop and skip.
Then Noah said, "Let's have a dance-
  contest
to see which animal dances best."

So chattering chimps and snakes alive
came on doing the jungle jive.
And the caterpillars said, "These guys are
  good.
We'd dance like that if we only could."

Then ants and bugs too many to number
came on doing the wriggly rumba.
And the caterpillars said, "That's a bit too
   quick.
We've too many legs and they're
   made to stick."

The frogs and toads put on some pop
and started showing the poolside hop.
And the caterpillars said, "Just look at them
   leap!
All we can do is crawl and creep."

Then bees from hive and bears from cave
came on doing the redwood rave.
And the caterpillars said, "What a buzz,
   what a roar!
There's no room for us on the dance-hall
   floor.

"The lizards can leap and the gerbils prance –
they're all doing the desert dance.
We love the rhythm and we hear the beat,
but we can't keep up with our caterpillar
  feet.

"And look at those birds as they chirrup and
  flap –
they're all giving us a treetop rap.
We like the action, we admire the sound,
but they fly so high, and we're on the
  ground."

So the caterpillars sighed as they sadly said,
"We can't join in." And they went to bed.
But they weren't there long before each
  little sack
began to open with a rustle and a crack. . .

And they came out looking like a prince and
  princess
doing the flutter in fancy dress.

And Noah said, "Brilliant! The butterflies
   have won."
Everybody cheered and out came the sun.
Then they all danced out with a hop and a
   skip
from Old Noah's Animal Dance-Hall Ship.

Willow Pattern

Willow tree, willow tree, why do you weep?
Is it for sadness, for sorrow?
The heavens are heavy, the waters are deep,
and the world reaches into tomorrow.

Willow tree, willow tree, what do you
  whisper?
Is it a secret to share?
The garden's a-rustle, the river's a lisper,
the breeze is a murmur of air.

Willow tree, willow tree, what is your tale?
Is it of loss and of love?
Who is the boatman and where does he sail?
And what of the bluebirds above?

Willow tree, willow tree, what is your
  answer?
Speak of your story, and true.
Willow tree, willow tree, sorrowful dancer,
sing me your song of blue.

You probably have in your home a plate or a saucer with this popular old pattern on it. Maybe, like this poem, you have wondered what the story is that it seems to be telling. Some people say there is an old Chinese tale behind the pattern, but other people say that the story was made up to make sense of the plate. In any case, I grew up not knowing the story, so this poem is about wondering why the picture on the plate seems so dreamy and sad. And wondering, too, what the story actually is.

Plum

Don't be so glum,
plum.

Don't feel beaten.

You were made
to be eaten.

But don't you know
that deep within,
beneath your juicy flesh
and flimsy skin,

you bear a mystery,
you hold a key,

you have the making of
a whole new tree.

Index of first lines